# I Want to be a Firefighter

### By Janice Behrens

No part of this publication can be reproduced in whole or in part, or stored in a retrieval system, or transmitted in any form or by any means, electronic, mechanical, photocopying, recording, or otherwise, without written permission of the publisher. For permission, write to Scholastic Inc., 557 Broadway, New York, NY 10012.

ISBN: 978-1-338-88863-8

Editor: Liza Charlesworth
Art Director: Tannaz Fassihi; Designer: Tanya Chernyak
Photos ©: cover: kali9/Getty Images; 3: kali9/Getty Images; 5: Mike295855/Getty Images; 6: LightField Studios Inc./Alamy Stock Photo; 7: George Shelley/Getty Images; 8: McIninch/Getty Images. All other photos © Shutterstock.com.

Copyright © Scholastic Inc. All rights reserved. Published by Scholastic Inc.

1 2 3 4 5 6 7 8 9 10   68   31 30 29 28 27 26 25 24 23

Printed in Jiaxing, China. First printing, January 2023.

# SCHOLASTIC INC.

I want to drive the firetruck.
Do you?

I want to put on the hat.
Do you?

I want to slide down the pole.
Do you?

I want to climb up the ladder.
Do you?

I want to spray the hose.
Do you?

I want to hug the dog.
Do you?